onederland

finding hope in the hard places

With love + hope ~
Elizabeth ♡

Elizabeth Maxon

Back Porch Press
CLEMSON, SOUTH CAROLINA

Back Porch Press, Clemson, SC 29631
www.elizabethmaxon.com

PRINTED IN THE UNITED STATES OF AMERICA

Library of Congress Control Number: 2017903464

Maxon, Elizabeth
        Onederland / Elizabeth Maxon 2nd ed.
        ISBN: 978-0-9987868-0-3

For Lucy, our Doodlebug

and all the other brave families living with chronic illness

lucy

The world is indeed full of peril, and in it there are many dark places; but still there is much that is fair, and though in all lands love is now mingled with grief, it grows perhaps the greater.

—J.R.R. TOLKIEN

A Note from the Author

In 2015 I published a compilation of stories called 'Type Onederland: Finding Hope in the Hard Places'. It was an e-book intended for distribution within the type 1 diabetes community. Within weeks of the release I began receiving emails and phone calls indicating that those stories were resonating with people both inside and outside of our community.

The message of 'Type Onederland' spread like wildfire not because it was a perfectly written book, but because it was an invitation for others to step into our story of grief and suffering. The pages contained **honesty** alongside **hope** – two things this world could always use more of.

One friend said it this way,
I so needed this book! I mistakenly thought it might not resonate with me because I have no loved ones with type 1 diabetes. I was so wrong! There is a universality to this message. I practically cried my way through it, not because it was sad, but because it touched me in so many relevant ways. This is one I will read again and again.

We all have our own 'hard places' and 'Type Onederland' became a way for us to share those experiences together.

Over the past year I have been invited to dozens of book clubs and events to connect with others who read these honest words of a desperate mama. I have sat in living rooms and auditoriums sharing my story and listening to yours. At every gathering tears are a guarantee. Tissues are always needed. Hope multiplies, when grief is divided. I'm not very good at math but I like that equation.

Because of the unexpected response to the first edition, we have re-branded and updated this collection of stories. This book, we are simply calling 'Onederland', will continue to connect us in our suffering. I hope the words that follow will slow us from racing through our struggles and encourage us to sit with our sadness for a bit. I hope the community that has formed will continue to grow as we collectively proclaim that that life is hard, but hope is here – right in the middle of it all.

One new addition to the book is something I call 'Insta-thoughts'. These are posts I have shared on Instagram that will give you a greater understanding of our everyday life with type 1 diabetes – the good, bad, and ugly. If you are on Instagram you can continue to watch our journey unfold by following @elizabethmaxon or searching for #typeonederland Feel free to use the hashtag to document your own journey and connect us to one another.

Thank you for joining us in Onederland. I think you'll like it here.

With love and hope,
Elizabeth

Out of suffering have emerged the strongest souls;
the most massive characters are seared with scars.
— Kahlil Gibran

{Lucy in her happy place - the original cover of 'Type Onederland'.}

Table of Contents

x

Introduction

Her name means 'light'.

When she was a baby she cried the hardest and laughed the loudest. I had friends with calm, docile children – the kind you might not even notice bundled up in their car seats, tucked under the table at the coffee shop where the mamas gathered.

Lucy hated car seats,
and high chairs,
and swaddle blankets,
and anything else that threatened to confine her.
Even her own skin, at times, seemed too restrictive. The brightness of her could never be contained or ignored.

From the time she could talk she was a storyteller. She would recount actual events with exaggerated hand gestures and animated facial expressions. She would dramatically create fictional adventures with academy-award winning skills. I am a storyteller too. Her story is one of my favorites to tell.

Sometimes the telling of stories must wait as we shift all of our energy into the living of them. In the weeks following Lucy's type 1 diabetes (T1D) diagnosis we focused all of our time and energy on learning how to live a new story.

As the shock of having a child with a chronic illness wore off, I began to face the reality that my story going forward would be very different than I could have ever imagined. Her story would be different, too.

It's one thing to grieve lost dreams in your own life. It's another thing to grieve them for your children. It is painful. It is cry-until-your-whole-body-shakes painful.

I never planned on sticking needles in her arms multiple times a day
or cringing every time someone offered her a piece of candy or

reading the labels on everything in the stinkin' store
or obsessing over the number on her blood sugar meter
or planning for sugar crashes that could leave her unconscious
or looking into her tear-filled eyes and telling her,
Yes we will have to keep doing this every day for the. rest. of. your. life.

I have been filled with grief. But the thing about grieving is that it is a process of letting go.

> **Sometimes our fingers must be pried off**
> **the dream of a good life**
> **so our hands are open**
> **to receive a better one.**

It's hard to believe that your 5-year-old daughter being diagnosed with type 1 diabetes (and a thyroid disorder) is a good thing. So I don't believe it's a 'good' thing. I believe that within it lies a better thing.

I believe that for reasons I cannot yet fully see
her life will be more significant,
her light will shine brighter,
her faith will root itself deeper,
her love will span wider,
her grace will stretch farther,
her Savior will hold her closer,
because her story took this turn.

I believe this because I believe Jesus meant what he said when he said...

*I came so that they can have real and eternal life, more
and better life than they ever dreamed of.*
{John 10:10 MSG}

Whatever turns our stories take we can be sure
*that in all things God works
for the good of those who love him.*
{Romans 8:28 NIV}

And so I love Him. With every turning of the page, with every chapter completed, I love Him.

So find a cozy spot and get comfortable. I want to share with you the chapters of our life we call ONEderland, because even the most difficult parts of our stories contain great purpose.

When the worst thing happens, it's never all bad.

#typeonederland

We all need the reminder that we're not alone, that we're not the only one dealing with whatever it is we are dealing with. These are Lucy's 'you're not alone' sisters. They know all about finger sticks and carb counting and insulin dosing. All of these girls have T1D but they also have each other and this mama is grateful.

CHAPTER ONE

Bad Dreams

She crept up beside my bed and whispered,
I had a bad dream mommy.

Normally I would have walked her back to her room, rubbed her back and kissed all the scary thoughts away. But that night I pulled back the covers and she climbed in beside me. I knew what the day ahead would hold and all I wanted to do was hold her.

Just hours earlier, I was downstairs on the couch balancing my laptop on my legs, looking for answers. I typed in all the symptoms we had observed over the previous three weeks.
Frequent Urination
Weight Loss
Mood Swings
Increased Thirst
I hit 'search' and every single result was the same.

Type 1 Diabetes.

I hit the 'refresh' button and nothing changed, but I knew

everything had changed. I couldn't move. I couldn't breathe.

As much as I hoped I was dead wrong, I knew in my heart I was completely right. An observant mama and Google can make a pretty good team when it comes to medical diagnoses. It was God's kindness and mercy that led us to put all the pieces together while she was tucked tight in bed - before the nod of a doctor's head made it official the following morning. But I wasn't thinking about all that then. I was too busy trying not to fall apart.

It was my husband, Joey, who set the laptop aside, grabbed my hand, and lifted me from the couch and to my knees.
We have to pray.

But once our hands were clasped and our eyes were closed, his mouth fell silent. Grief had him in a chokehold. I willed the words to come out of my tear stained face. I tasted salty water as I begged God to be light in this darkness. I offered my child to his strong arms as my own frame grew weaker and weaker.

I don't know how I slept at all that night.

They say a normal blood sugar level is between 80 and 100. When they performed a simple blood test at the pediatrician's office Lucy's was well over 400. By the time we were admitted to the hospital that afternoon it had exceeded 500.

Type 1 Diabetes.

Lucy learned the term that day. Unless a cure is found, she will live with the disease for the rest of her life.

I've always known my children would face struggles in their lives, but I didn't know it would be something so big that began so young. Skinned knees and broken hearts are one thing, but a lifetime of finger sticks and insulin injections was something entirely different. I felt my heart cracking under the weight of this reality.

I had spent months preparing to speak at a women's retreat that very weekend. I had three messages prepared to deliver to an auditorium full of women. On the day I was scheduled to step into a retreat center I was stepping into a hospital room instead. I didn't understand.

God made no mistake when He took my hand and led me to a very specific place in His word just weeks before. It turns out, the truth I uncovered wasn't preparation for the message I would deliver, but for the season I would enter.

Though the theme of the retreat was 2 Corinthians 5:17, I kept coming back to the beginning of the chapter. It was the opening verses that kept speaking personally to my heart, and I didn't understand why until that day.

For we know that when this earthly tent we live in is taken down (that is, when we die and leave this earthly body), we will have a house in heaven,

*an eternal body made for us by God himself
and not by human hands. We grow weary in our present
bodies, and we long to put on our heavenly bodies like
new clothing.*

*For we will put on heavenly bodies;
we will not be spirits without bodies.
While we live in these earthly bodies, we groan and sigh,
but it's not that we want to die
and get rid of these bodies that clothe us.
Rather, we want to put on our new bodies
so that these dying bodies will be swallowed up by life.
God himself has prepared us for this,
and as a guarantee he has given us his Holy Spirit.*
{2 Corinthians 5:1-5 NLT}

And so I grieved over the condition of her earthly body
and the weariness she felt curled up in that hospital bed.
But the calm came swiftly on the wings of a belief that is
rooted in my soul – a belief that our troubles here are
temporary, but what is coming is eternal. The best is
always ahead. The knowledge of that brings hope.

*So we are always confident, even though we know that
as long as we live in these bodies we are not at home
with the Lord. For we live by believing and not by
seeing.*
{2 Corinthians 5:6-7 NLT}

Always confident.

The words rolled easy off my lips when I told her this -
It's going to be hard, Doodlebug.
This diabetes thing won't be easy, but remember how we always talk about God's plan for our lives? Don't forget, he is writing a story with your life and this is part of it. He is in all of this. You can trust Him.

You can be confident.

It's hard being away from home. I would have much rather been tucked in my bed instead of sitting in the hall on that cold hard hospital floor. I would have rather seen her in her own bedroom surrounded by stuffed animals instead of on the other side of that door surrounded by doctors and monitors.

But something happened then and there. My desire for home grew. My appreciation for it magnified.

I am learning to live well here until I eventually get back there – to my eternal home.

Yes, we have bad dreams, and sometimes those bad dreams become reality, but

You won't see us drooping our heads or dragging our feet! Cramped conditions here don't get us down. They only remind us of the spacious living conditions ahead. It's what we trust in but don't yet see that keeps us going. Do you suppose a few ruts in the road or rocks in the path are going to stop us?

When the time comes, we'll be plenty ready to exchange exile for homecoming. But neither exile nor homecoming is the main thing.
Cheerfully pleasing God is the main thing,
and that's what we aim to do,
regardless of our conditions.
{2 Corinthians 5:6-9 MSG}

Sometimes we forget. Sometimes we get bogged down and discouraged. But on our good days we live in the light of that truth, and it keeps us going.

When you decide to make the 'main thing' in your life something that isn't dependent upon conditions or circumstances - that changes everything.

#typeonederland

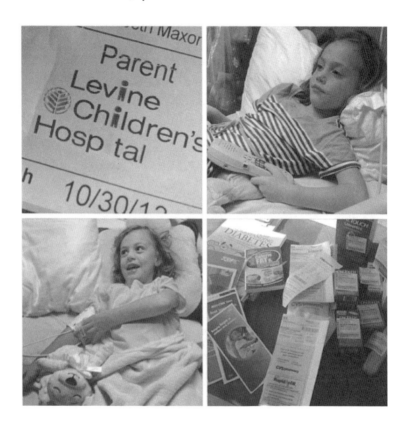

Goodbye hospital. Hello new life.

CHAPTER TWO

Held

That first week was a whirlwind.

As the world seemed to crumble around me, hands pressed in from every side keeping me from breaking apart too.

When you are adjusting to a new life in which you
inject needles into your daughter's arms five times a day,
and draw blood from her little fingers before every meal,
and set an alarm to wake and check 2am blood sugar,
and count carbs to calculate insulin dosage (did I mention I am NOT a math person?!),
and juggle the emotions of a 5-year-old with a lifelong illness and a 3-year-old who is getting less than his fair share of attention,
you need someone who is not currently drowning to throw you a life preserver. You are desperate for that person to come alongside you and hold your hand and remind you that everything will be alright.

For us there were countless hands that came in the form of texts, emails, phone calls, meals, balloons, gifts, caring for the kids, tight hugs, shared tears, fervent prayers and words of truth.

And our family was upheld.

In their war against the Amalekites the nation of Israel was guaranteed victory only if Moses remained with his hands raised in the air holding the staff of God. When his hands fell, his people began to lose the battle to their enemy.

Holding up a nation in crisis is hard work. Holding up a family in crisis is hard work too.

At some point fatigue sets in and you grow weary and it becomes more than one or two people can bear. Moses reached that point and in that moment he felt hands pressing into him.

> *Aaron and Hur held up his hands,*
> *one on one side, and the other on the other side.*
> *So his hands were steady*
> *until the going down of the sun.*
> {Exodus 17:12 ESV}

With their own hands, and in their own ways, our community of family and friends steadied me. From the rising to the setting of the sun, and all the dark hours in between, I was never left alone with my weary arms struggling.

Raised arms are less a sign of strength and more a signaling towards the source of our strength. It is a form of praise in the midst of suffering. Our community came alongside me to hold them up, raised to the God I love, the God who always brings victory. That victory belonged not just to our family, but to all those who stood beside us in battle. We all need our people – our arm holders.

Many brought presents in those early days – balloons, cards, coloring books, stuffed animals – but it was their presence that was most important to us. Meeting someone else's needs doesn't have to be a major ordeal. Sometimes the best thing you can do is show up.

As we watched every need met through the kindness and generosity of others I realized that even before we knew we would need that strong support system, it was being built up beneath us.

One such strong place was my friend Mary.

The day before we would receive the official diagnosis, Mary and I sat together on a playground bench. What seemed at the time to be an impromptu play date after preschool was actually a divine appointment. As we watched the kids swinging and sliding I spoke aloud for the first time my concerns about some of Lucy's symptoms. At the time I had no idea what could be causing them. Was it a bladder infection? Was it normal 5-year-old behavior? Mary and I considered all of the questions and concerns together.

On that first night when I put everything together and got my answers from Google, it was Mary I texted first, through tears of grief. I just knew we had that conversation earlier in the day for a reason, and she was already positioned in my life for that time and purpose.

One week later we sat together again. This time it was at her kitchen table and instead of a conversation full of questions it was a conversation full of tears. Our children were swinging and sliding outside just like many days before but for me, for our family, everything was different. Mary gave me a safe place to process all of that. We talked and cried and I thanked her for all she had done in those fragile early days.

She practically adopted our son, Oliver, into her family while we were at the hospital. She offered her prayers and support over and over again. She made herself available every single moment, regardless of what was happening in her own life. But most importantly, she carried the weight of it all with me.

My sweet friend had been given a heavy burden for what we were enduring and though I was sorry to see her broken over it, I was also grateful she did not try to crawl out from underneath it and run away. She stayed hunkered down right beside me through every grueling bit. I know she saw straight through my flesh to my broken mama heart and somehow, almost supernaturally, she felt it all too. Others had different roles, but this was Mary's and I am grateful she accepted it.

It is a gift to have someone who doesn't just see your grief completely, but who wedges her own fingers beneath it and lifts it up so that, side by side, you can begin moving forward.

In that season I needed someone who didn't have all the answers and was comfortable enough to ask the questions with me.

I hope you have people in your life like my Mary. I also hope, when given the opportunity, you will be as brave and courageous for someone else, as my friend was for me.

There is no protocol for how to respond to a family in crisis. There are no magic words or standard courses of action. Each person has a different role to play and a different need they can meet when crisis hits.

In our story, I am confident there are many people I could not even name because their contribution was made through silent prayer and anonymous action. Their part was no less important to me than the ones whose faces we saw daily. For every person who spent even a moment entering into our suffering I am grateful – for the holding and the carrying they did.

#typeonederland

These are the numbers of type 1 diabetes. Lucy woke me at 3am to tell me she was really thirsty and had gone to the bathroom twice. Sure enough her blood sugar was high...after a low 62 before bedtime. It was a long night of drinking water, going to the bathroom and rechecking sugars but we are back to normal this morning and I am incredibly grateful for a 6-year-old who knows her body.

CHAPTER THREE

Thanks

Normally, I don't like to rush through the week of Thanksgiving, but that first year we were all ready for the twinkling lights early. The kids spent the day before Thanksgiving examining each ornament and placing them in just the right spot. The handmade ones with crumpled edges, holes and cracks were lovingly hung with even greater care than all the rest.

Since both kids were less than four feet tall at the time, you can imagine what the finished product looked like. I managed to get a few shiny things placed up top but I didn't have the heart to move theirs around for the sake of an evenly ornamented tree.

That night when we turned off every light in the house the glowing tree looked perfect. Oliver stared, as a soft grin stretched across his face.
What do you 'fink' mommy? Isn't it beautiful?

Even when things are messy and uneven and have holes poked clear through them, the right light has a way of making it all beautiful. So we take what we've been given and hold it in our hands like a treasure. We find the perfect spot to put it on display. We take extra time and care with the broken and battered pieces because we know they have a story to tell too. As difficult as it may be to look at them in their imperfect form, we begin to see them as perhaps the most important part.

That night we prepared our hearts for Thanksgiving. There is the *thanks* and there is the *giving*. It's easy to say we should be thankful, but we sometimes forget to give thanks for what has been given - *all of it.*

That year our family had been given
happiness and heartbreak,
delight and death,
sacredness and sadness.

We received shiny new treasures and had precious possessions crumpled and torn away right before our eyes. Still, we chose the same response as every other year.
In all things we give thanks.

We give thanks for that which we asked for and that which we desperately hoped would pass us by.

When we see every bit is meant as a gift
our burdens become blessings,
our hard places begin to make us soft,
our weakness uncovers true strength,
and the things that broke us apart actually bring us closer together.

When Lucy, in her princess nightgown, invited us all to dance there by the tree, no one hesitated.
Daddy, you dance with Mommy.
Oliver, you dance with me.

With Frank Sinatra crooning in the background we wrapped arms around one another and danced in the lights illuminating our imperfect tree and our imperfect life. With my face pressed against the face of my beloved, I watched the children spin and twirl and I couldn't stop smiling and quietly giving thanks for every bit of joy and suffering that had led our family to that place.

We don't need a special holiday to celebrate with a thankful heart. In every season of life my prayer for all of us is that we will position every piece of our lives in the light of the One who makes it all beautiful - who makes every gift a good one - and give Him thanks.

CHAPTER FOUR

From Grieving to Giving

Some stories seem more like a work of art than a series of events. It's hard to paint that kind of picture with paltry words. When you set feet on holy ground the words don't come easy, but I've decided it's better to tell a good story inadequately than to never tell it at all.

This is a good story.

We were at my in-laws lake house when I got the text. I read the words once, twice. Still the disbelief remained. I spoke them aloud to Joey making the situation slightly clearer in my mind.

Type 1 diabetes was still new to us. Lucy was still calling it 'diafetes'. Before she was diagnosed I did not know a single child with T1D. Almost exactly one month after we were discharged from the hospital I found it so hard to believe that our little world suddenly included one more.

My friend Amy was on the other end of the text that night. Just a couple of weeks before, her family had been at my house. They saw our new life of blood sugar checks and insulin injections. I detailed for her all of Lucy's symptoms and the series of events that led us to the hospital. Her family was part of our strong support system.

On that post-thanksgiving day, all of that information suddenly came in very handy for Amy. Her sister, Anne, was in town visiting from Washington DC for the holiday. Anne and her husband had three children. At the time, the youngest was five - just like Lucy. His name was Ford and, according to the text, they had just taken him to urgent care with the same symptoms Lucy had displayed a month earlier. Hours later the diagnosis would be official - type 1 diabetes.

It was late but I called her anyway.

When I heard Amy's voice on the line the tears pushed their way up. I listened to her relay the story of her nephew and every bit of what we'd just climbed out from under fell heavy on me again. I could hardly believe I had already found myself on the other side. I was already looking at another family's grief and seeing my own.
Just like that.

Sometimes the greatest gift we are given in our grief is to be the gift to another.

My body and soul had been wrung out so dry I felt like I might dissolve into nothing. Suddenly all that nothing could be something to someone else.

As we drove back into town I explained to Lucy -
*There is a little boy named Ford. He is five just like you.
He was at the hospital just like we were and has just found
out he has diabetes too. Remember how we were sad and
scared and not sure what to do at first? I bet that's how he
is feeling. We are going to help.*

She was ready. It's an amazing thing to be able to help
when you yourself have felt so helpless. We stopped by
the store on the way and, without hesitation, Lucy began
choosing things for the friend she had not yet met - a
stuffed dog, some favorite low-carb snacks, and a funny
card.

I will never forget walking along the sidewalk up to Amy's
house. It was dark and cold. Christmas lights were
flashing from the neighbor's yard. Ford stood on the front
porch, waiting, as Lucy approached with gifts in hand.

He spoke first in a tiny but strong voice.
Hi. I have 'diabedience' too.

Lucy looked at me, puzzled, as if to say
*Wait a minute, he has 'diabedience' and I have 'diafetes'.
That's not the same.*

I smiled and quickly interjected.
You must be Ford. Yes, you and Lucy both have diabetes.

This is the part where the words break down and I wish I
could strap you into Marty McFly's DeLorean and take
you back with me.

Back to the moment I saw his small frame and big grin and knew all too well the war raging in his body.

Back to the moment when Lucy looked him in the eye and handed him the card she had carefully chosen.

Back to the moment when I wrapped my arms around his mama and a thousand unspoken truths passed between us.

Back to the moment we sat down together - father and mother alongside father and mother - to pour out our collective grieving hearts.

Back to the moment when I listened to my husband honestly recount his struggles, and yet offer heaping piles of hope up in his hands.

Back to the moment when I called it what it was - so very hard - and all of our eyes glassed over because we understood completely.

Back to the moment when two little brave ones each grabbed their bag full of medical supplies and sat down at the table next to each other.

Back to the moment when three families circled around them and watched as she taught him how to prick and check all by himself - and he did.

Back to the moment when they each realized they were not alone.

Back to the moment when even the grown-ups were reminded - *we are not alone.*

I wish Lucy didn't have diabetes.
I wish Ford didn't either.

But there is a truth that has been solidified for me on this journey.
> **the things that take us to the depths of despair also take us to the depths of the One who overcomes that despair.**

The One who overcomes it all. In this world we face trouble. Jesus has a response for that.

> *Take heart. I have overcome the world.*
> {John 16:33}

That night, at my friend's house, the ground beneath our feet was holy because in that place Jesus was overcoming. He was overcoming our pain and our sorrow and our loneliness with something more powerful - Himself. The weaving together of our lives wove us closer into Him.

It's why He came to be *with us.* Immanuel. God with us.

Ford could have received his diagnosis on one of the dozens of days when he was back home in Washington

DC instead of the handful of ones he spent in North Carolina. It was not only a gift for his family that it turned out the way it did, it was a gift for ours too. Times like those are a rare opportunity to see the plans of heaven gently unfolding in front of you. They are a sweet reminder that every bit of it carries meaning and purpose.

That night four grieving parents huddled together with little ones on arms and legs, speaking prayers and shedding tears, because the trials of this life are so stinkin' hard, and at the same time so incredibly sacred.

Just when fear seems to have you in its grip you realize that a slight shift of letters - of perspective – changes *scared* to *sacred*.

Sacred means something connected to God,
something not of this world,
something that deserves our reverence.

When our weary hands lay those trials down at His feet He transforms them into something sacred. Something not of this world, that connects us to Him, and deserves our reverence.

Sacred is difficult to describe, but unmistakable when experienced. It's why I wish you had been there. I wish you could have experienced the connectedness of two broken families,
the opportunity for our nothingness to be offered as something,

the reality that in this world full of trials and despair we are not alone because He is with us.

> *When we see the image of God*
> *where we don't want to see the image of God,*
> *then we see with eyes not our own.*
> - Richard Rohr, "Everything Belongs"

#typeonederland

She spent all morning traipsing through the woods, sledding, laughing, and playing with her brother. It wasn't until we were back home that she said she was feeling low and I watched her little shaky hands check her blood sugar. 37 - the lowest she's ever been. I can't believe she wasn't passed out on the floor. No complaining. No drama. She just had some juice and a cupcake and was good to go.

CHAPTER FIVE

A Secondary Diagnosis

It's hard to hear big ugly words coming from such a small beautiful place.
I HATE you mommy! I do not like you at ALL! I wish you were NOT my mommy! And I wish I didn't have a BROTHER either!

Sticks and stones break your bones...
and what was that part about words never hurting? The hate- filled words of your child break more than bones.

I guarded myself from their meaning early in the morning. It wasn't the first time I'd seen them coming like arrows for me. By the grace of God, a deep breath, with eyes closed makes their penetration into my heart less painful.

It's only a matter of minutes before the attacking screams turn to repentant cries. And the roller coaster ride barrels on.

The day after Lucy was diagnosed with type 1 we found out about another autoimmune disease. In addition to the emotional impact of a new life with T1D, we also began facing the reality of hormonal swings and a myriad of other problems associated with thyroid malfunction. At the time, her secondary diagnosis was Graves' Disease. Whenever it took hold of her I tried everything to bring peace and calm back to her spirit. Sometimes I held her. Sometimes I rocked her. Sometimes I hugged her. Sometimes I sang to her. Sometimes I just had to leave her alone screaming in her room.

Later we would talk about how it could have gone better, knowing that the same sequence would repeat itself again before the week's end. Always I would wrap her up in unconditional love and limitless grace I promised to offer every day, all the time. I whispered silent pleading prayers that it would be enough to heal the wounds in both our hearts.

Initially the identification of Graves' disease seemed like a minor sideshow, but it quickly took center stage. The doctor told us almost as if it were an afterthought.
By the way, her thyroid hormones are also elevated so we are testing her for Graves' disease.

I was already so overwhelmed with the learning curve that comes with T1D so I kept this additional information tucked away in a separate compartment of my brain until I had the capacity to open it back up and understand.

When the Graves' diagnosis was confirmed I took the bottles of pills they gave me and figured out how to slide them down her throat in a puddle of yogurt. I assumed the latest of her autoimmune disorders would wait patiently in the corner while I got a good handle on the one right in front of me. I was wrong. This one didn't sit quietly. This one demanded my attention with sobbing and yelling and fits of rage. I quickly realized it was a box of explosives I had so naively set to the side. Hormonal imbalances in a five-year- old are no joke.

I write many words about grace but I want to tell you that we were daily living it - the receiving and the giving. At some point we must practice what we preach and what we have heard preached. Otherwise, it will evaporate and leave nothing lasting behind.

That season of my life made me desperate for God's grace. In this time and place in which we live we are not desperate for much. This life of privilege we live is a blessing but, if we're not careful, it becomes our curse. When you live in a world where you can pretty much get anything you want with a credit card and a smile, you start to feel like you don't need anyone or anything else. That lie slowly lulls us to sleep until a desperate situation wakes us back up again to this truth.

Desperation is the fertile ground upon which our faith grows.

It just might be the craziest prayer we ever pray, but it also might be the most important.
God give me a desperate heart.

In the place where I come to the end of myself –

where I don't know what to do,
where I have no control,
where things are beyond my understanding,
where I am desperate, I plead for grace.

I beg for it to stand guard over my lips, and bring gentleness to my eyes, and hold still my hands and heart. And it does.

There have been seasons of less stress in which I have snapped, and lost my ever-loving mind, and lived full of regret. Yet this one was ushered in with winds of peace. In my desperation I have watched my faith in myself grow small as my faith in God has grown big. My reserves would have long since dried up, but by His power we flourish like a well- watered garden.

What do you say? Might we be brave enough to step together onto the shaky ground of desperation and watch faith grow right before our eyes? Might we be ready to stop avoiding desperate situations or trying to plow through them as fast as we can? Might we instead allow for the discomfort of the things we cannot change to change us?

The comfortable seasons of life lead us to see Jesus as we imagine Him to be; but these days of desperation? They take us beyond imagination to the truth of who He really is - everything we need.

God give me a desperate heart.

May we have the courage to seek and find the desperate places in our hearts.

May the breaking apart lead us to wholeness again.

May we run toward, not away.

May the dry places be flooded with living water.

CHAPTER SIX

Back to Life

Type 1 Diabetes has required sacrifice from us all. In the beginning, we felt like it would drain us dry.

When your world is rocked, the unstable ground beneath your feet seems to indicate you may never walk forward with ease again. It is difficult to imagine getting back to any semblance of the 'normal' life you once lived. And yet we must get back there. When other important things become, well, *important* again – it is a gift.

Months before our days in ONEderland began, I heard about an event I wanted to attend. I set a reminder on my calendar to buy tickets the day they went on sale. I never do that, but this event seemed important for me and the work I was doing as a writer. Then something *super weird* happened.

The day I was expecting to receive the email about purchasing advance tickets, one of my email accounts stopped syncing to my phone. I was away from my computer all day and didn't realize what had happened until I got home that night. Once I realized, I held my breath and got onto the event site as quickly as I could only to find the tickets were all gone. Sold out.

I was so disappointed, but then I remembered –
whenever something *super weird* happens there is usually
a reason.

So I decided to be a big girl, and let it go.

**I've learned that sometimes God
has to interrupt my plans to make room for His.**

One month after being disappointed by that missed
opportunity we were completely devastated by Lucy's
diagnosis.

When we received the news that set our lives into a
tailspin my protective mother instincts immediately
kicked in. I began eliminating every responsibility or
engagement that could possibly interfere with my
focusing 100% on helping our family survive. If that ticket
had been in my possession I would have sent it right back
from whence it came, because I was not going to let
anything get in the way of this mama on a mission for her
baby.

When crisis hits, it's hard to imagine you will ever have
the capacity to do anything else for, like, <u>forever</u>. You
can't imagine when you will actually be able to
reintroduce yourself to the world. You can't even be sure
all the pieces of the life you had before will fit into this
new reality. But I didn't have the ticket, so I couldn't do
anything stupid with it.

44

One month after we checked into Levine Children's Hospital and began learning about insulin injections and pancreatic islets, one month after my heart and mind shifted their focus entirely onto that one thing.

One month after I quietly cried myself to sleep in that tiny hospital bed snuggled tight against my girl.

On the one month anniversary of Lucy's diagnosis I cried myself to sleep again.

This time the tears were full of gladness instead of mourning.

Emily emailed on a Tuesday to say she had a ticket for me – that ticket I missed out on the first time around, that ticket to join a small group of dreamers, writers, singers, grace-givers, ordinary people with hearts for uncovering extraordinary life.

At the last minute one had come available. Of course it had. I could almost see her hand extended towards me with a piece of paper reading, 'admit one'. It had been held for me. It had been reserved until the last minute when I would barely be ready to say 'yes'. It was placed in my hand just as I was coming up for air.

Breathe in. Breathe out.

Sometimes the trials we face seem to steal the very breath from our lungs, and we stay alive only because we are being given mouth-to-mouth resuscitation. We wonder if we will ever be able to breathe our own breath - our own life - again.

One month earlier I had been ready to release every dream I ever had for my own life to preserve the dreams I have for my daughter. But God said 'no'. He did not require that sacrifice.

All the ways I create art with words and thoughts and connections and stories and people - He could have taken them. He could have left me without an ounce of time or energy left for any of it. Yet right there, in the middle of a life not going according to my plan, I began to see his plan more clearly. That plan involved being the mama of a little girl with type 1 diabetes but it also involved something more.

The morning of the event I woke up early, slipped on my cowboy boots, took a deep breath and began to understand how that new, still-fragile life, was actually strong enough to hold all the dreams He's set in my heart alongside all these responsibilities He's set in my hands.

Do you know that fragile feeling? Maybe you've lived it. Maybe you are living it right now. If so, hold on. Don't throw your dreams out of the window just yet. There is still room. You may not be strong enough to hold it all together right now, but He is. Underneath all those fragile feelings something stronger is being established.

I pulled into the gravel lot at a picturesque barn just a few hours from my house. From the moment I arrived everything said 'welcome'. Lights were strung, tables were set, food was prepared. I had forgotten what it felt like to have something prepared for me. I had forgotten the importance of letting others take care of me in the midst of all my frantic care-taking. I gave the tears of gratitude a chance to fall before getting out of my car.

Once inside the wide open, yet cozy, space of the barn I sat down at a table full of strangers. We immediately began chatting and getting to know one another. I struck up a conversation with the couple seated next to me. Within moments, I could feel the needle moving in and out of our hearts as the shared stories began to knit our lives together.

I unpacked the details of Lucy's diagnosis, which led us down the road to their own child's medical emergency. Our tears came together into one shared pool for parents who know what it means to stand over a sick child realizing you have no control over the prognosis. The symptoms were different but the experience was so similar.

Heads nodded and shook as we examined the ways our stories overlapped, and opened our hearts to reveal what could now be found in those wounded places. We asked questions and shared answers. We admitted when there were none. We brushed back the mess of our lives to reveal the bright truth and beauty that had grown up underneath it all.

I realized, then, that our new story wasn't replacing our bigger story as a family, it was being woven into it, making it more vibrant and true. The crisis would not stop us from moving forward, it would actually propel us to new places and new people.

Eighty people came together that Saturday to consider what it means to create art. But, as I watched, something almost magical happened. The art was created right there among us.

Our smiles and laughter painted big bold strokes of color to fill the space between us. A sweet, haunting melody was born of our tears as we reached deep in our souls and pulled out heartache and fear.

When we face crises and life looks differently than we thought it would, I don't think it's an indication that we are to shut down forever. Yes, we may need to hunker down temporarily, but shutting down is not necessary.

I had a wise friend give me some good advice the week after Lucy was diagnosed. *Don't make any major life decisions right now.*

It's true. Our grief compromises our judgment. Our tears make it too difficult to see clearly what lies ahead. When crisis comes, we hunker down but we don't shut down. We keep the little light of our life blinking, on hold, until we can get back to it. When we do, we find it deeper, wider, and stronger than we ever could have imagined.

#typeonederland

Lucy and Dr. Nelson - her endocrinologist.
We love him and all the other medical professionals who
have been such an important part of our journey in
Onederland (special thanks also to Hello Kitty for
carrying Lucy's insulin pump/pancreas for her :)

CHAPTER SEVEN

The Digging Times

With freshly laundered dishtowels in hand I walked downstairs to find Joey sitting alone in a quiet kitchen staring at the wall. When I asked what he was doing he said he was *just thinking*. I pulled up a chair across from him in silence. After a few moments I asked,
What are you thinking?

Tentatively he responded,
I'm not sure.

Rather than prodding, I waited. I knew the dots were not connecting with ease, and there may be some pieces of the picture being unearthed in his head and heart. I've been there.

What followed the silence was a conversation about living in the digging times. We didn't call it that. We discussed struggling through change. We lamented over living without clear direction. We asked a lot of questions and couldn't find the answers, despite all the words we exchanged.

In the digging times, I often find myself with dusty holes all around me and nothing valuable to offer - no finished product. Nothing seems to connect or make any sense. Something beautiful and productive can be born from digging times, but always the digging must come to an end and we must come back to ourselves.

I often have questions about how to parent
or what kind of diet our family should follow
or how I should handle a particular situation
or what my role is at work
or how I should spend my time
or what I should write about.

Unlimited information is available to us with the tap of a finger anytime, any day. I so often set off, determined to find the answers to all my questions by digging
in books
and websites
and YouTube videos
and social media
and magazine articles
and the advice of friends
and the opinions of experts
and before I know it, I stand up and look behind me to find a trail of holes that have led me far from where I began.

At some point the digging has to stop and I have to stand up, dust off my hands, and turn around. If I'm not careful, what began as helpful begins to harm. I can dig myself so deep down into information that it's hard to find my way back out.

At some point I have to acknowledge there is plenty more information I could unearth, but it will only lead me further from home. At some point I have to rely on my own two feet to take me where I need to go. At some point all the doing of digging must give way to being and belief.

In the early days following diagnosis I wanted to know everything about autoimmune issues. I had to be careful not to let a healthy awareness turn into an overwhelming obsession. Sometimes learning about something brings more fear than freedom, so I learned to set boundaries and trust God to lead me to the right people and places. He did.

If, like me, you find yourself covered in dirt and weary from the searching, maybe it's time to pause. Maybe you've done enough digging on this matter and it's time to sit alone in a quiet kitchen and let things come together in their own time. Maybe it's time to take the shiny valuable pieces you have found so far and offer them up, leaving the worthless ones behind.

And always, always, make sure your deepest hole is dug in the Truth. In my own experience, making room first for God's word and his instructions for me will always position me in the right place when there is digging to be done.

CHAPTER EIGHT

Delayed Reaction

The tears streamed down, and I let them flow as freely as
they would, making of them a pillow for my heart.
On them it rested.
- Augustine

I walked in the house with my arms piled full of trash from the car. It's amazing how we automatically move through the simple tasks of our days in the middle of crisis. Sometimes it's the only thing holding us together.

The kids were on my heels. I dumped everything in the garbage can and headed for the side table in the living room. It held the closest box of tissues. He saw the tears, still fresh on my cheeks, and I'm sure my face was red and tired. I couldn't make eye contact or I would erupt again. I didn't trust myself to speak.

Joey cried the hardest in the days following Lucy's diagnosis. I cried too, but the bulk of my tears didn't come until months later.

I've had friends with kids who are plagued by chronic health conditions. As a school psychologist I worked with families who received devastating diagnoses. In every case my experience lasted only moments, maybe hours. I could always walk away from it. Not anymore.

On that particular day, it surrounded me. When I woke up in the morning. When I was cooking breakfast. When I was driving to the store. Chronic illness lives with me now. It promises to stay forever. When something difficult moves in and doesn't have any plans to leave, it can be hard to keep the flame of hope alive. There is always something to put it out.

I am high on empathy. It's a great trait for someone who works with people. It can be hard for a mama. Empathy means you absorb the emotions of other people and experience them as if they were your own. When you have a child who demonstrates every emotion imaginable in a 5-minute span, that's a lot to absorb. It's hard to wring it all back out. Sometimes you walk around heavy and sopping wet all day long. Oh, to feel lighter.

In the middle of a struggling season we often give ourselves a pep talk. We try to stay positive. We focus on all that is still good and true in the world. I highly recommend all of those strategies, but on some days we need a different solution. On that particular day, I didn't need to escape my new reality, I needed to learn how to endure it - with hope. The dying needed to happen to make room for this new life. As painful as it was, I needed to die.

I tossed the tear-stained tissue in the trash and went

upstairs. locked myself in my bedroom and let the sorrowful music play. It was the words of Audrey Assad that wrapped themselves around me.

Bring me back to life,
but not before you've shown me how to die.

Instead of ignoring my heart and trying to silence the wailing sadness, I needed to let it be heard. I needed to feel it completely -
the pain,
the fear,
the grief,
and the deep, deep sadness over our condition.

By 'our condition' I mean 'our' condition - yours and mine. Broken hearts are the result of a broken world. For me it was the burden of a child with a chronic illness for which there is no cure and no clear course of treatment. For you it might be something else, something that leaves you all heavy and sopping wet.

Whatever our condition is, we have to feel it completely. We have to be brave enough to do that. We have to step into the pain so that it can kill us completely. Nobody wants to walk around half-dead, hanging on by a thread, covering it all up with a smile and a cute new top we bought on sale at Target.

I stood in the shower with my eyes closed and the water, mixed with my tears, pouring down. I listened to the truth of the words being sung knowingly, and I died. It was

57

deeply painful, but it gave way, bit by bit, to hope.

When you find a safe place to unravel, when you feel the arms of eternity wrapping tight around you - you stay. You don't run and hide, or turn and fight. You stay there.

It is not a time of rejoicing.
It is not a time of rising.
It is not a time of being resurrected.
It is not a time of boisterous triumphant victory.
It is a time to mourn.

It is a time to be held.
It is a time of surrender.
It is a time of dying, so eventually you can live again.

In that season, we were still figuring out how to live with type 1 diabetes. We still didn't have a handle on Graves' Disease. We were spending the majority of our time visiting different doctors and trying different therapies and swimming in questions without answers.

I had to apologize daily for her hitting or punching or yelling or just giving an evil death stare. I was not apologizing for her, for who she is. I was apologizing for the way disease manifests itself. I was apologizing for how it detonates like a bomb inside of her and then sends shrapnel flying into anyone close to her.

I am closest to her. I got the most hits. I took them

because it's what I was set here to do. To be her
defender,
protector,
advocate,
caregiver,
nurturer,
and most of all,
the great big flashing arrow pointing her to Jesus. The
One who is enough when I am not.

I can say He is the great hope of this world all the livelong
day, but in that season I had the chance to live it. I
grabbed desperately onto the truth that He is the only
person in the history of the world to actually overcome
the world. Boy did we have a world that needed
overcoming.

Overcome with peace,
with relief,
with healing,
with mercy,
with grace,
with an eternal hope.

I am part of an on-line support group for mothers of
children with chronic illness. There are nearly 150 of us in
the group from all over the world. I have never met a
single one of them face to face but they understood more
about the battle I was fighting than anyone else. We
gather in a safe, virtual space typing in letters on a

keyboard to form pieces of our hearts - our weary, breaking hearts. I don't mean to sound gloom and doom but many days are that way for us.

These are some of the words I've seen poured out in that space.
I'm a mess right now.
Trying to pull myself out of this depression.
I feel so distant from my family because they don't understand this is a real thing.
I had to pull my daughter out of school.
This is such a rocky road.
I have reached my breaking point.
I cried so much today.

You don't need any experience with chronic disease to have said some of those same things. Our struggles may be different but the emotions are the same.

That same dying day, Lucy snuck downstairs after her bedtime and stood close waiting for my typing fingers to pause. I looked at her with soft eyes and smiled. Her cheeks were pink from the day's sun. Her freckles looked to have doubled. Her eyes were questioning when she said –
I didn't mean to make you sad today Mama. I can't go to sleep because I'm sad I made you sad.

I propped her little chin up on the tips of my fingers and guided her face up to mine. I looked deep into her eyes

60

and told her.

You make me happy. You make me smile. You don't ever make me sad. Mama wasn't sad because of you today. I was sad because sometimes life is hard. Sometimes we have bad days. Sometimes I get upset that you have to deal with all this diabetes business, but I always have hope. I always trust God. I always believe he will bring something good out of this.

And then, for some crazy reason, I told her the story of Jehoshaphat.

She listened. The questions in her eyes turned to answers. She didn't say a word, but I know she heard it all.

I told her about a great king who faced great opposition. I explained how despite overwhelming odds, God fought for his children when they cried out to him; how victory in difficult times comes not from us but from him; how God uses us in the middle of our saddest, scariest times to point others to Him and His power; how all of this is possible because of God's great love for us; and how he promises to never leave us, even when we are dying.

I know she locked it all away. That's what she does. She puts my words in a treasure box inside of her. I have to make sure they are something worth treasuring. She will bring them out another day, and for that I am so grateful. She always hears me. Above the sound of Graves' rage and the roller coaster of fluctuating blood sugars, she hears my voice. She hears the truth. One way or another, it will set her free. It has set me free.

It's been years since those tears came like a flood to drown me. Our life isn't perfect but we are alive. We are full of hope. We are free.

The battle has been won, not <u>by</u> us, but <u>for</u> us.

Jesus himself showed us what it means to endure,
when you want to escape.
There are some things well worth dying for.
{Luke 22:42}

#typeonederland

I'm speaking at the TypeOne Nation Summit today. My girl and I got up before the sunrise to be with our people. I cried twice within 10 minutes of arriving. When you're with your people...it can be emotional.

CHAPTER NINE

Interior Design

We were laying side by side in her bed. I had just read the part of Laura Ingalls Wilder's story where Almanzo's mother squeezes through the dining room door in her hoop skirt to present the platter of ham for a big family dinner. I don't know if it was the idea of family being together under one roof or if her mind had already wandered back on its own. Whatever led her there, she snuggled up close to me and whispered,
Mommy? Do you think that man is still there?

It took me a moment to find my way onto her train of thought.

Earlier in the day the kids and I had gone to the North Carolina Transportation Museum. After hours of climbing on locomotives and checking out covered wagons just like the ones Pa drove on the prarie, we made our way back toward the entrance. As we rounded the corner past the picnic area Oliver was the first one to spot him.
Look! That man is taking a nap on a table.

I glanced up and across the grassy field that separated us from the picnic shelter. Sure enough, on top of one of the tables was a man dressed in gray with a long shaggy beard to match. His eyes were closed and his head was resting on a duffle bag that likely held all of his possessions inside.

Oh, honey, I think he is probably homeless.

Without hesitation Lucy suggested we take him some food. We've done that sort of thing before and she, of course, remembered. I agreed it was a good idea and said we would see if he was still there after the train ride we were hurrying to make.

We got busy and forgot.

That night, Lucy remembered. Laying cozy under her soft covers with her mama reading her to sleep she thought of the one whose bed had been a bench of wood. When I looked at her I saw the glisten of her eyes and the deep sadness they held. Her words confirmed what was in her heart.
It makes me sad to think about him, Mama.

We talked about what happens when our hearts are moved to sorrow for someone else and what we can do in response. In this case we agreed to pray together for that man. We locked hands and did just that. We considered the ways God might answer our prayers by leading him to a homeless shelter or sending someone else to give him food. I could tell she felt better but not completely. It wasn't until I suggested we find a local homeless shelter where we could serve that I saw her move toward contentment. She didn't want to talk about it. She wanted to do something.

I knew she would ask about it the next day. Guaranteed.

Compassion is the sympathetic concern for the suffering of another. Lucy has compassion. I had completely forgotten about that man, but she was still carrying a burden for someone she didn't even know.

She was six years old at the time.

Six year olds say things like,
Hey, that's mine!
No fair - he got more than me!
When is it my turn?!

On occasion those words have graced Lucy's lips too. But more and more often I hear her say caring words.

A six-year-old with compassion.

I don't think I have taught her that. I actually believe it has been set inside of her tender heart by other hands. I also believe that her journey with type 1 diabetes has created within her a fertile ground for such things to grow and bloom. Seeds are sown in suffering. All I can do as her mama is acknowledge it,
make room for it,
and direct it to action.

It's a sacred moment when you see something in your child that you know is too good to have come from anything you have said or done. It is a double gift when you realize the ways that goodness has been born of suffering. In those moments all we can do is hold our breath and pray for the words to create a space for the stirring and movement of Spirit to continue.

I wonder how many of those moments I have hurried right past. I implore myself to pay closer attention to what is happening in that fertile soil of the tiny hearts I tend. I'm so grateful God is at work in that space, in every space. I'd hate to think of the weed-filled garden that would come from the work of my hands alone.

CHAPTER TEN

Lessons from a Princess

I watched a mother and daughter walking out of an ice cream shop with treat in hand and smile on face. They looked so happy, so carefree.

I stood there with the lump in my throat that warns of tears. It was two months post-diagnosis. I had gradually shed more and more of the anxiety, grief, and bitterness associated with our T1D life, but at the time I was struggling.

On that particular day I envied a mother and daughter for being able to indulge in such a simple pleasure without concern for how much insulin would be needed or whether the dairy would cause further damage to her immune system or if any of the ingredients had gluten hidden in them. I felt like my carefree mother-daughter relationship had been hijacked.

Writing was a challenge back then. Every time I began, it went in the same direction and I wanted to drive that bus somewhere else. I didn't want to bore others with more details of the latest test results or share my fear of introducing tofu into our diet or agonize over the dozens of different theories I was reading about the causes and treatments of autoimmune disease.

Most of all, I didn't want to come across as
obsessive
or radical
or frantic
or looney-bin-bound.
But I was.

I was so hesitant to trust myself with words. I kept waiting on myself.

Waiting to finally get my act together.

Waiting until I had a perfect course of treatment to implement.

Waiting until I could prepare the new meals with ease.

Waiting until I didn't hold my breath for every single blood sugar check.

Waiting until I didn't spend every waking moment thinking about my daughter's health.

Waiting until I had completely gotten a handle on this 'new' life.

You see what I meant by obsessive, don't you?

Even in the waiting I had to do something, so I began writing again. I had to step forward, however timidly.

We had made it through the Christmas holidays so I began looking ahead to the promise of a new year. The truth was, our new year came early that year - our new life.

Sometimes we don't want new but we get it handed to us anyway. Sometimes our lives feel just about right thank you very much and we are happy to keep things as-is. And yet we are forced to accept a gift that at first seems more like a curse. I was reminded of Sleeping Beauty. Lucy loves that story.

Before she was Sleeping Beauty, she was Princess Aurora. I bet her mama had big dreams for that little baby. At her christening, fairies came bearing special gifts. The first two fairies brought gifts of life. Flora offered beauty. Fauna offered song. Before the final good fairy, Merryweather, could wave her wand, the evil Maleficent stepped in to bestow her own offering - death by spinning wheel.

Fairytales always have a dark side, but they rarely end in darkness. Merryweather still had her chance, and in light of Maleficent's evil curse she offered up something very specific to the princess child. Instead of falling into death on her sixteenth birthday Aurora would instead fall into a deep sleep - a sleeping beauty.

Shortly after the debacle of the christening, Aurora's mother had to say goodbye to the life she had dreamed of with her daughter. The girl was sent away in an attempt to hide her from harm, but one day she would return and live her happily ever after.

Sometimes new life involves loss and heartache, but there is always another offering that follows. Our happily ever after is still ahead.

Maybe you are being pushed into a new season you hadn't planned on. Maybe you are saying goodbye to one that was filled with all kinds of 'new' you didn't ask for. Either way, something is being offered to you.

As you breathe in the air of today you may carry a little hesitation, but let's remember together that there are brand new days in front of us. Each one of them contains an offering. Some will feel like a curse but each will move you closer and closer towards the kind of 'new' that is being made in you.

Even when the darkness floods in, there is a gift of light coming. We look for it. We keep moving through the waiting even if there are bits of bitterness and grief in our pockets. We take steps forward.

Just like Princess Aurora, those things that seem to promise death can be transformed into something that actually brings life - a new life you might never have expected but that feels just right once you get it all the way on.

#typeonederland

Look who's featured on Beyond Type 1!

CHAPTER ELEVEN

Overcoming Addiction

Imagine a cold dark room in the basement of a church. Imagine we are all seated in those brown folding metal chairs. Imagine I stand up out of mine and walk to the front of the room and turn to face you.

Hi, my name is Elizabeth and I am an approval addict.

Don't laugh. It's true. It took a lot of guts for me to stand up and say that to you. I have spent my life caring way too much what other people think about me. An approval addict's greatest fear is this - someone not approving of them.

It happened to me.

I've always tried to be a low-maintenance person. I've been accommodating and willing to bend some of my own preferences to let others have their way. My reward for that has often been approval. When you're addicted to approval, you'll do anything to get it.

After Lucy was diagnosed a shift took place. I realized that I would be the expert on her disease and the way she managed it. I realized that I was going to have to make some decisions and draw some lines for her benefit that may inconvenience, or even offend, others. It was hard, but it was necessary. Suddenly my desire for approval was trumped by something else. I was more concerned with doing what seemed right and in the best interest of my child. I only wish I had come to that realization earlier in life.

Because Lucy was diagnosed with more than one autoimmune disease, her treatment was complicated. We chose to do some things that others didn't necessarily agree with, like eliminating certain foods from our diet, trying alternative medicine, seeking out chiropractic treatment, and changing the overall way our family ate.

I was hit hard by some disapproving words from some people I love and respect. Has that ever happened to you? Maybe, for you, it came in a face-to-face conversation or via email or over the phone or from someone who overheard a conversation about you.

For me, it felt like the worst thing, and yet somehow it became the best thing. Taking those hits of disapproval was like taking arrows right in the heart. I felt like I just might bleed out and die. Then something miraculous happened - I survived. The breath was still in my lungs. The blood still pulsed through my veins. I was alive, and maybe more so than I had been before.

When I don't receive approval I feel small and worthless. If I follow those feelings I wind up in a ball in the corner of my closet dying a slow death. If, instead, I follow Jesus

I slowly stand up and pull the arrows out of my heart and watch immediate healing take place. I experience new life inside of me.

That day I had the choice –
follow the feelings or follow the truth.

I am ashamed to say that in the past I have chosen to follow my feelings far too many times. I have chosen to feed my addiction and make decisions based on what will make others happy rather than what I believe is best. This time was different. This time it was about my child. This time my behaviors being called into question were ones I felt confident about. This time I had poured prayer and wise counsel all over the decisions I was making. This time I clearly saw a Savior hand reaching towards me and I clasped it tight and let it pull me back up on my feet.

I thought to myself,
Sometimes even an approval addict is willing to sacrifice approval for something she really believes in.

And God said,
Sometimes? Really?? Sometimes? The things you believe in - the things I have called you to do - they should always be more important than what someone else will think about you.

Ouch. He's always butting into my private conversations with myself.

I really shouldn't joke because this is serious business. I

had a moment. I had a my-life-will-be-forever-changed moment. I suddenly came face-to-face with the real danger of being an approval addict. If I didn't sacrifice my need for the approval of man I would be of no use as a servant of God and I would neglect my responsibilities as a mother. Wow. Talk about a painful reality check.

How many times have I missed something God had for me because I was too focused on doing the things that would earn me the approval of man rather than the pleasure of God?

Don't get me wrong. There are times in life when serving God will get you the approval of others. That's great. But that can't be our motivation, because there will be other times when serving God will leave you unapproved and unpopular by everyone else's standards.

If you're an approval addict too, your worth, like mine, is found in the opinions of others instead of your identity in Christ. When you begin making decisions based upon that assumption you are in dangerous territory. You are also setting yourself up for exhaustion. You may be able to play the approval game and gain credibility and likability and all the things that allow you to advance in life, but you can only keep up that act for so long. You will never make all the people happy all the time.

At some point we've got to stop trying. What do you say? From now on when God calls us to something let's be brave enough to forget about what everyone else is thinking and focus completely on pleasing Him.

That is obedience.
That is surrender.
That is humility.
That is punching our own foolish pride in the face.
That is the freedom that comes from serving Christ alone.

Living with a child with type 1 diabetes has taught me that.

God whispered something to me during my addiction recovery. I want you to imagine him looking at you with grace-filled eyes and saying them to you too.

If you think you've found success through the approval of man, just watch and see what you can do when it's my approval alone you seek.

CHAPTER TWELVE

Drowning

I took dozens of beautiful pictures during our family beach vacation. My Instagram feed from that week would leave you smiling and envious –
grinning kids building castles in the sand,
the sun reflected in the waves just beyond my blue painted toenails,
perfectly plated seafood dinners,
colorful buckets full of shells and sharks' teeth.

The pictures represent pieces of that week - happy, smiling pieces - but they do not tell the complete story of the big jumbled pile representing the incomplete puzzle of my life in that season. There are other pieces that would not have been so pretty to look at.

On rare occasions a drowning person actually needs the pounding waters. Breathless, I made my way to the coast, to the water. I arrived there drowning in
doubt
fear
franticness
anger
frustration

sadness
the voices accusing me of being an unfit mother
the medical questions looming unanswered
the responsibilities left unfulfilled
the deafening noise a season of crisis projects like a bad
set of speakers turned all the way up.

Sometimes the things that drown us go virtually unseen
by anyone else. That's the part that really stinks. That's
the part that leaves you feeling so desperately lonely.
Everyone else sees the pretty pictures while we feel the
ugly truth that
life. is. hard. and nobody seems to notice that we're
drowning.

Somehow the lifeguards have all gone off-duty. They took
a break for 'adult swim' and suddenly here's an adult who
has forgotten how to swim. There is nobody to save her -
to save me, to save you.

I tell my kids daily to *use your words*. And so I try to use
mine to say -
I'm having a really hard time.
I think I'm about to lose it.
This whole situation has become almost unbearable.
I need help.
I don't know what to do.

But somehow even those honest, vulnerable words
couldn't convey the war zone in which my head and heart
were dodging bullets every hour of every day.

That night I sat in my pajamas on the porch that faces the shoreline. As the sky grew dark I began to feel light again. Sometimes the drowning things need to be drowned out. Sometimes they need to be washed into deeper waters like the little plastic toy my son Oliver had lost to the waves that week - carried away in the instant it was dropped.

If I carry the suffering alone too long the weight of it starts to take me under. That night I began releasing some of the heaviness. As I did, I began to feel myself doing more floating and less flailing. Even though the drowning things still remained I closed my eyes
to the sound of the waves crashing loud and rhythmically,
to the brush of wind blowing strong and thick,
drowning out...
drowning out...
drowning out the drowning things.

These drowning things - what are they for you?

Write them down. Say them aloud.

They are like splinters lodged in your soul and it's time you realized that the source of all that pain was something so small and fragile that you could snap it in two with your fingers.

The hands that carved the shores for the seas,
the lips that blow the winds where they please,
are greater than every drowning thing that has been dragging us deeper and clinching us tighter.

I used to believe that the best way to see your own problems as smaller was to focus on the bigger problems of others, but now I know better. Our problems don't shrink in the shadows of bigger problems, but in the light of
bigger grace
bigger truth
and a bigger God.

I will never have all the answers about Lucy's medical condition and everything else any mama worries about. I will always battle questions of
How did this happen?
Could we have done something to prevent it?
Is there a better way to help her?
Am I missing something?

But sitting my small self alongside the vast ocean and breathing slow and steady somehow made the questions seem smaller and less scary, as the God of the universe revealed himself bigger and more beautiful.

#typeonederland

My people. Team Maxon.
Type 1 impacts all of us and we are in it together.
We are 100% behind our girl 100% of the time!

CHAPTER THIRTEEN

Fragile: Handle with Care

I have this hand-painted, blown-glass Christmas ornament. It is so fragile and beautiful that every year I hold my breath as I remove it from the red velvet box and display it on the tree for everyone to see. To hold it too loosely, or too tightly, would be to destroy it.

That's how I felt about our trip to Chicago. I feared that wrapping words around it might cause the whole thing to shatter into tiny unrecognizable pieces. But it is a beautiful, fragile chapter that needs to be told.

I left for Chicago in search of healing for Lucy. I returned as the one healed.

At the time we were in a fairly good groove with the T1D, but the Graves' disease continued to wreak havoc. Because the original diagnosis and proposed course of treatment never sat well with me, we had been on a long journey of searching for more information and different answers. That search led us to Dr. Qin in a small Indiana town just south of Chicago.

Back then Lucy was having her blood drawn every month to measure thyroid hormones and antibodies. We sent all of her blood work to Dr. Qin and scheduled an appointment for him to take a look at Lucy and propose an alternative course of treatment. When we arrived at his office he greeted us with a smile and looked over all of Lucy's most recent lab work. He asked us many questions, conducted a thorough physical examination, and then Dr. Qin suggested that either Lucy was misdiagnosed with Graves' originally or she had recently gone into remission. There was also the chance that she may have developed another thyroid condition called Hashimoto's.

On the one hand it was the greatest news because we had hoped and prayed for remission. We had tried all sorts of alternative therapies and dietary changes to increase her chance of it. On the other hand, some of her antibodies were still high which indicated something was still off with her thyroid. According to Dr. Qin, the bottom line was that Lucy's immune system was still malfunctioning on multiple levels. Things were looking better and there was no need for any of the previously recommended surgeries or procedures, but we still were not completely sure what was going on. In my mind I still saw the tiny interior of her body like a war zone. It frightened me.

Dr. Qin recommended no treatment for her thyroid at that time and a continued monitoring of her hormone levels every three months. He was very encouraging. He said that Lucy looked healthy and her body appeared to be coping well with multiple autoimmune issues. He did not, however, have any answers or suggestions for me about one of my biggest concerns - Lucy's severe mood swings and their accompanying behavior.

When I received no insight in this area, I realized that was what I had most hoped to achieve during the visit. I was desperate for a plan to do something about the catapulting back and forth between anger and sadness that she experienced on an almost daily basis. It was hard to walk away without a solution. Autoimmune diseases can be so complicated. Parenting kids can be so complicated.

I walked out of Dr. Qin's office that day satisfied that we had found a good doctor, and encouraged by his analysis of her condition. At the same time, I was devastated that her body was definitively fighting against itself on multiple fronts and discouraged that we didn't have any easy answers about the emotional roller coaster ride we were on.

It was all I could do not to burst into tears, but I held it together and tried to force down lunch with a smile at the local café near the hospital. After lunch, I drove our little bright blue bullet of a rental car back into Chicago, dropped it off, and the two of us made our way to Shedd Aquarium as I had promised Lucy we would. She was so excited. I still felt nauseous.

Hand-in-hand we walked across Grant Park stopping to examine flowers and pet puppy dogs. With every step my mind slowed it's racing a bit. I watched her wide eyes drinking everything in once we entered the giant building and as we went to take our seats for the featured show.

I cried silently straight through the entire thing.

It wasn't that the dolphins' performance was particularly moving. It was just that it was the first chance I'd had all day to sit down quietly with her cuddled up next to me and let the tears catch up. They had been chasing me down since I walked out of the doctor's office, biting at my heels.

I sat there on that concrete step of the Oceanarium Auditorium, with beluga whales splashing in front of me, and let myself pull back to see a bigger picture. Because of that change in perspective the tears wound up being born of love and not fear. For that I am grateful.

The ones that would have fallen earlier in the day would have been full of lamenting. *Her body could be killing off another gland? Now we have to pay attention to signs of adrenal failure too? What if there is even more damage going on that we don't know about? How are we ever going to make any changes and improvements if there are no more tests run? What will I do now that I don't have an answer for her* extreme emotionality?
I don't know anything.

But the tears that ran soft and warm hours later spoke differently. They spoke straight truth instead of some twisted version of it.

I'm holding my little girl full of life and light.
I've taken her on a big city adventure for the first time in her life and we have made precious memories.
I know her.
I know that she won't budge during this show because she is mesmerized by animals of any kind.
I know she loves chocolate and stuffed animals and riding her bike and creating art and having her back scratched and singing songs and dressing up like a princess.
I know who she is - autoimmune issues and all.
And I love her so completely.
<u>*I know her.*</u>

In the midst of all the unknowns it was a comfort to remember that. I may not know everything but I know her. No one knows a child like her mother. It is a precious and holy gift to possess the greatest earthly knowledge of another person. Equally precious was the realization that God knows her even better.

He Created her.
He sees every cell of her body.
He sets a unique purpose in front of her.
He knows what she needs and what she is needed for here on this Earth.
He will do with all of this what he chooses, regardless of my meddling and interference.
<u>*He knows her.*</u>

Later that night at the hotel we indulged in something special, something we typically try to avoid because of Lucy's diabetes. Giddy with excitement, we decided to

order some famous Chicago pizza, put on our pajamas, and eat dinner in bed! As I picked up the phone to call, she looked up from the iPad she was playing and set her eyes on mine. Her grin spread ear to ear.
I bet I know what you're gonna order, Mama!
Mushrooms and tomatoes!

And I did.
She knows me too.

It's what it means to be family. It's what it means to journey through this crazy, messed-up life together. To know and be known by that precious angel-spirit of a girl suddenly felt like the greatest of all treasures that I held -
Carefully,
Not too loose,
not too tight.

Hold on.

Lucy's thyroid issues have continued to come and go over the years. It is difficult to know which issues are related to which diagnosis. Those who live with, or love, someone with type 1 diabetes will not be surprised to hear that some of the mood problems remain even when thyroid levels are normal. Although they are much less severe, swings in blood sugar leave a person feeling rotten and sometimes they take it out on those closest to them. In those fragile moments we just keep hanging on to what we know. I hope you will too.

#typeonederland

Chicago with Lucy.

CHAPTER FOURTEEN

Strength in Weakness

There was a night the week we got home from the hospital that Joey had to hold her down. All three of us were on the floor of our foyer right next to the skinny wooden table with the flowers carved along the side.

My dad bought that table for me on a trip we took to San Francisco many years ago. I remember the truck unloading it onto my front doorstep two weeks after I returned home. I excitedly tore into the box only to find it in pieces - completely broken apart and beyond repair. It was like someone had dropped it off the back of the truck and run over it. It would never work for holding the lamp and framed pictures I planned to set on top of it, and so I returned the broken table. They sent me a new one a few weeks later. This time it was in one piece, beautiful and strong and capable of holding things.

That night, on the floor next to the wooden table, she was crying and screaming at the top of her little 5-year-old lungs,
No, no, no! Please, no!

I was crying too, holding the needle in my hand. Joey held her still long enough for me to shoot the insulin into the back of her arm and hold it - 1, 2, 3, 4, 5...and done. I handed the needle to him and scooped her up onto my lap - both of us still crying but slower, quieter now. She buried her head in my shoulder. We had only been home from the hospital a couple of days and all of us were emotional wrecks.

A younger version of me would have never imagined a scene like that playing itself out. It's not part of the dream you have for your children. It's not even something I thought myself capable of doing before Lucy was diagnosed. And yet, within a couple of months it became as routine as brushing our teeth.
Peel the paper off the needle.
Screw it onto the top of the insulin pen.
Remove the big plastic top and then the tiny green one.
Test the needle to make sure it's working.
Do the math in your head - blood glucose correction plus carbohydrate intake.
Dial in the right amount of insulin.
Pinch the back of her arm.
Stick the needle in.
Count to five.
Pull it out.
Dispose of the needle in a sharps container.
Repeat at the next mealtime.

The whole process eventually became so automatic that it's hard to remember it ever being such an ordeal, but it was. She asked me that night how much longer we would have to do the shots. How do you explain to a five year old that she would never get a break? How do you tell her that the carefree child life she lived just days before was over and the need for insulin injections would never end? How do you communicate that this is not a temporary treatment but a lifelong lifestyle?

We used over 3000 needles in our first 20 months of type 1 diabetes. When you do something that many times, you get the hang of it. But I never stopped wishing we didn't have to do it.

Lucy is adopted. Before we became her parents we had to fill out mountains of paperwork. One of the forms asked several questions about what issues we were willing and able to handle as adoptive parents. Joey and I felt comfortable with nearly all of the conditions, except one. We both agreed we were not equipped to handle a child with medical needs. Of course at birth, Lucy did not have any apparent medical needs. But five years later we were faced with the one thing we thought we couldn't face.

Every night at bedtime, as I am turning out her light, she says the same thing.
Come and check on me. If I'm low give me something yummy.

And every night I do. I don't need the reminder. I never forget. A few hours later, just before my own bedtime, I creep in with her meter and pull her small hand out from under the covers and pick a finger to prick. If the numbers are good I cover her back up and kiss her one last time. If they are too high, I calculate how much insulin she needs and administer it. If they are too low, I wake her up and she gets something 'yummy'. If I can't get that number easily back under control, it's a long night.

I am not a creature of habit. I rarely do the same thing, the same way, twice. I am forgetful. I lose my keys on a weekly basis. I honestly cannot be counted on to brush my own teeth every night and morning. I am messy, not meticulous. I see the big picture, but miss the details.

A daughter with diabetes has required me to be something I am not and to do things I do not feel capable of doing and to overcome emotions I did not want to feel, and so for that I have had to stretch and grow and depend on a power greater than myself.

That night we spent crying on the cold, hard floor I felt like the table that had been delivered in pieces. I was in pieces. I was broken apart. I did not feel fit to do the job expected of me. I was unable to hold myself up, much less anything else. I felt like I had been dropped off the back of a truck and run over.

Can you relate?

There were moments when I wondered -
Why God? Why would you give this child to me? Why

would you put me in charge of this situation? You know how you created me. You know how difficult this will be for me. You know there are other people who would be able to do a better job. What if I can't be all she needs me to be?

But something happens when you have used up all of yourself and it's not enough. In that place you find out there is something besides self that will sustain you.

And so I began to sense God's response to me -
Yes, I know. It is difficult for you. Others could probably do it more easily. You feel weak and inadequate and that is good, because at the end of your own strength is where you will find mine.

Instead of being rendered useless.
Instead of being returned and replaced.
I was transformed. I was changed.
Not because of something I did, but because of something I could not do.

I'm not sure why it is that we wait until we have tried every little trick up our own sleeve, and it doesn't work, before we draw from a deeper well.

> **Circumstances require us to change,**
> **but something in our souls**
> **that is not of ourselves**
> **makes that change possible.**

When you see yourself become something you never

thought you could become, it is evidence that there is more to yourself then - well, yourself. That is a precious, holy, and sacred thing.

There is no significant thing that I have done or will do that was not sourced from somewhere deep in my soul. Those depths are not reached by easy everyday choices. They are reached by difficult, not-what-I-signed-up-for, circumstances.

I was given the gift of a handicap
to keep me in constant touch with my limitations...
No danger then of walking around high and mighty!
At first I didn't think of it as a gift,
and begged God to remove it.
Three times I did that, and then he told me,
'My grace is enough; it's all you need.
My strength comes into its own in your weakness.'
Once I heard that, I was glad to let it happen.
I quit focusing on the handicap and began appreciating
the gift. It was a case of Christ's strength moving in on
my weakness. Now I take limitations in stride,
and with good cheer, these limitations that cut me down
to size—abuse, accidents, opposition, bad breaks.
I just let Christ take over!
And so the weaker I get, the stronger I become.
{2 Corinthians 12:7-10}

When life is hard it helps to know there are people out there who understand. Lucy has said for years that she wants to be a chef. Recently she has become a big fan of @chefsamtalbot who not only is an awesome chef but also knows how hard life can be as a type 1 diabetic. Chef Sam has become one of our heros because he's committed his life to making delicious food and using his platform to help those like Lucy with T1D. Tonight Lucy is perusing his cookbook for some culinary inspiration but what we are really hoping for is a chance to go visit his new restaurant @prettysouthernbk in NYC... wouldn't that be 'sweet'?!?

CHAPTER FIFTEEN

Just What We Needed

After twenty months and 3000 needles, we decided to transition Lucy to an insulin pump. Instead of giving her multiple injections from a small needle every day we chose to insert a port under her skin every three days using a slightly bigger needle.

I put that decision off for months. I wasn't sure we could handle another change. I wasn't sure I would be able to make the necessary adjustments. Quite frankly, that big blue contraption used to inject the port into her skin scared me to death. I was scared I would do it wrong. I was scared it would hurt her. I was scared I would mess up so terribly that she would refuse to wear a pump ever again. I was also scared the pump might malfunction or she might accidentally punch a button that would inject too much insulin that would cause her death. Parents of type 1 diabetics carry a lot of fears and the introduction of the pump seemed to open the door to a whole slew of ones I wasn't prepared to face.

But here's the reality – all parents carry fears. All parents play out scenarios in their heads that end in some tragedy for their child. It sounds dramatic, but at least for mothers, it's a reality. I was facing fear as a parent long before we had a child with a chronic illness. This is what I had already learned about fear - it is not the boss of me.

Fear can be an *indicator* but it must not be given permission to be a *dictator*.

When we first began managing Lucy's diabetes with injections we had no choice. If we did not do what we were trained to do at the hospital our daughter would die. Twenty months later I was fairly confident in my ability to monitor blood sugar levels and administer insulin. The thought of trying something different was daunting, even if many others had raved about the benefits of making that change.

Once we were in a relatively stable season, our entire family committed to transitioning Lucy to a pump even though there were still fears and unknowns. I began to pray the words that have become my 'go to' when I feel called to do something that I'm not sure I'm ready to do. It's ridiculously simple and also ridiculously effective.

God, give us what we need.

At times like that we don't even know what we need. We didn't know what life would look like on the other side of using an insulin pump but we knew God would be there and we knew he could make provisions for us.

In the weeks leading up to Lucy's pump start date I read articles and connected with other parents and asked questions in preparation. Much of that was helpful but I still felt like we were lacking something. On the day of our first pump training class Lucy got cold feet, which left me feeling apprehensive and nervous too. I was putting on a confident face with her but I had an honest conversation with my dear friend, Paige, about my concerns.

Paige does not have a child with T1D and couldn't tell me a thing about pumps or inset devices, but something immediately came to her mind when I shared my honest fears. She remembered the daughter of another friend who has type 1 diabetes. Paige put me in touch with Matti. It turns out, Matti began using a pump at age 7, just like Lucy. It turns out, Matti was a college student who lived right up the street from us. It turns out, Matti had saved all of the colorful little pump pouches her grandmother made for her over ten years earlier. It turns out, Matti was just what we needed.

The week before Lucy's pump start date I called Matti. She eased all my mama worries. She offered to meet us on pump start day to help Lucy. Later that same day, my friend, Paige, called and offered to fix lunch for all of us as a special pump day celebration at her house.

On the scheduled day, we woke up early and drove 45 minutes to Lucy's endocrinologist office. As we traveled I thought about what the day would look like. I prayed my simple prayer again – God, give us what we need. I knew when we arrived at the office they would help us to begin

and then we would leave with this child who has an autoimmune disease that will kill her if untreated
and this device that was new and foreign to us
and these instructions that seemed so complex
and I knew we would be okay.

I was confident not because of anything I am capable of doing. I was confident because my weakness has given way to a greater strength. I was confident because I knew God would give us everything we needed, just as he always has before.

Matti showed up that day offering smiles and hugs and a gift for Lucy. She showed us how to get air bubbles out of the pump tubing and told stories of her own experiences with Type 1. We all ate lunch together at my friend's house where her children had designed and displayed colorful signs for Lucy. We sat on the back porch smiling and laughing and marveling at the way God meets our needs in extravagant ways. Before we left, Matti ran home and found the giant Ziploc bag full of pump cases she had saved and gave them to a beaming Lucy. It was just what she needed.

If someone had asked me to develop a perfect plan for that day it would have looked different. Thank goodness I was not the author. God penned it perfectly because He knows and loves us perfectly. We may not know what the future holds but we know that He holds it. And in His hands are all the elements necessary for the story He is telling with our lives.

His chapters are always so much better than anything I would have written. When I ask God to give us what we need, more times than not, he gives us more.

#typeonederland

Sometimes something extraordinary happens on an ordinary Tuesday. Sometimes you ask God to please help you get through something challenging and then he goes and pulls that 'abundantly more' thing where he doesn't just get you through it, He provides over and above what you even thought to ask for. Allow me to introduce you to Lucy's new pump and her new friend Matti (who also has T1D and started her pump 13 yrs ago when she was 7 just like Lucy). Not only did we make it through pump start day, but Lucy would say it was one of her favorite days ever.

CHAPTER SIXTEEN

A Regular Girl

It's the most magical place on Earth. Or so they say.

Living, breathing princesses, a giant grinning mouse, and whimsical rides through fairy tales. We had been enchanted all day long, but when we returned to our cabin at Fort Wilderness we were wiped out. Planning and executing a Disney adventure is not for the faint of heart.

Just as we were about to fall into bed it happened. Lucy's insulin pump malfunctioned. If I didn't find a solution for the problem quickly Lucy's blood sugar would continue to climb and we would risk her winding up in some strange hospital in Florida.

I did not handle it perfectly. Not even close. I got frustrated, did some huffing and puffing, and probably stomped and rolled my eyes a time or two. I could have landed a role in a Disney show with my performance. Fatigue seriously compromises my ability to handle inconvenience with grace.

When I walked back into the room where I had left Lucy

laying on a bench, waiting, I found her falling apart. Fat tears streamed down her face. It wasn't frustration I saw there. It was genuine sadness. My clinched jaw released and I felt the burning behind my own eyes as I knelt down and wrapped her in my arms.

Oh Honey. It's going to be fine. We can fix it. Mommy should not have overreacted like that.

And then silently, I pleaded that prayer, *God please give us what you know we need – right here, right now.*

Her big eyes were pouring as she looked up at me and her words tumbled heavy like river rocks out of her mouth – *I wish I were regular. It just doesn't seem fair.*

She said it not as a spoiled brat who wants to get her way but as a child who was wearily standing face to face with a harsh reality that hurt.

What words could I offer? How could I reframe fairness for her? How could I explain that this wasn't a punishment? How could I convince her that she really is regular? I kept asking questions about what I thought she needed in that moment but God answered my prayer and cut right through all my misguided ideas and gave me the answer. His answer. It wasn't what I expected because it wasn't what I thought was needed. It was what he *knew* was needed.

He carried me back to story after story we had read together in her bed at night. Stories of people like Moses, Esther, David, Peter, Mary, and Paul. I remembered each one of them were far from 'regular'. The words came streaming out of my mouth but they were sourced from a much deeper place than my own mind. They came from the deepest wells I had dug into his Word over the years. I gathered her up on my lap with her head resting up against my chest. When she was a baby it was the only position that brought her comfort when she was hysterical. Seven years later it was still my best shot at soothing her. I rubbed my fingers deep into her hair and said,

Lucy, I want you to listen very closely. Ever since you were a tiny little thing there is something I have known about you.

You are not regular.

God never intended for you to be regular. He intended for you to be so much more. Think of all the stories you have ever heard about the people God has used to do amazing things. Were any of them regular? Didn't they all have something difficult they had to overcome? Didn't God use the very thing that caused them to struggle to ultimately bring about something good, to do something important?

Her body softened and her tears slowed their flow as she listened to the rhythm of my words. When I paused she nodded her head up against me and quietly said,
It's still not fair.

To which I responded,
I know. It doesn't have to be. It's faith, baby. It's believing God's best is coming even when you're feeling your worst.

Living with type 1 diabetes is hard for Lucy. It's hard for our entire family. It always will be. My words won't ever change that, but the truth of who she is, and *whose* she is, make a difference.

I need those truths to make a difference not just for her, but for me too.

I love my daughter. I hate that she has to deal with these everyday burdens. If I'm honest, I also hate that I have to deal with them. I cringe thinking how selfish that must sound. But I must be honest about my selfishness. If I want to move past that line of thinking {and I do} I have to identify it first. I get irritated that managing Type 1 Diabetes takes up so much of my life. Some days I don't think I can spend another moment or ounce of energy managing it, but taking a break is not an option because keeping my daughter alive and healthy is my priority.

That's that.

My fatigue, and occasionally my hormones, will guide my feet awfully close to a sea of bitterness if I'm not careful. The only way I can save myself from drowning and taking the rest of my family down with me is to do something simple, yet difficult. I force myself to turn around until the toxic waves lapping at my feet are behind me and then one step at a time I walk away.

Away from selfishness and closer to selflessness.
Away from resentment and closer to redemption.
Away from fear and closer to freedom.
Away from those dying times and back to life.

I intentionally turn down the volume on the voices telling me
It's not fair.
You messed that up again.
You'll never get it right.
How are you going to continue living this way?

As those words grow faint and distant I press my ears up against the door of hope and listen for the life-giving words on the other side proclaiming,
I am a mama.
I have a little girl.
100 years ago she would have died from the disease she carries, but today there is treatment.
I am grateful for insulin.
I am grateful for doctors and nurses.
I am grateful for insurance.
I am grateful for healthy food.
I am grateful for photo ops with princesses.
I am grateful for every day of her.

Most days I don't live under the weight of it, but I do always live with the awareness that an untreated low blood sugar could leave her unable to wake up and an untreated high blood sugar could leave her organs failing, or worse.

There are other families who have watched what we currently hold in our hands yanked right out of their possession. Some have seen undiagnosed T1D lead to diabetic ketoacidosis {DKA} causing permanent damage and sometimes death. Others have found their children who seemed to have T1D well under control unconscious in their bed.

When the fatigue and hormones start talking and telling me that I will never get MY stuff accomplished and this life with T1D is not fair and I'm not doing it right anyway and, actually, I'm probably a complete failure as a mom and everything else I attempt. When that happens, I have to talk back. Even if I don't feel it in the moment I have to say what I know to be true. So do you.

No, it's not fair that our family has to live with chronic illness, but life isn't about being fair - or being regular. It's about being grateful. It's about carrying hope alongside the suffering. When I take a good look around I realize that being 'regular' is overrated and I am surrounded with opportunities to be and do so much more. Here's to embracing an irregular life.

CHAPTER SEVENTEEN

Out of Nowhere

I closed my head in the car door.

You read that right - my head. Not my finger or my arm or my foot, but my HEAD. For the record, this is not something that often happens to me. In fact, of all the hundreds of times I have gotten into a car this was the first time my head was injured in the process.

The kids and I had been at the neighborhood pool for 4 hours so maybe the heat was getting to me. In any case, I got them situated in the back of the van, placed a towel on my own seat and proceeded to hop in like I always do. At the last second, as I was pulling the door closed, the towel slipped and when I lifted myself up to grab for it BAM! I hit my head on the door frame. Then, as if that wasn't bad enough, I felt the weight of the door slam into the other side of my head too.

It hurt. I cried. I felt disoriented. The kids passed me their stuffed animals as an offer of comfort. It took me a couple of minutes to compose myself and then, despite the pain,

I realized I was ok. I wasn't great, but I was ok and I was going to make it.

There was a knot and bruise on my forehead. Fortunately, it was on the side of my head covered in bangs. No one else could see it, but I knew it was there. It was tender and continued to throb off and on for a couple of days. I went on about my daily life because, really, I was ok, but it still hurt like the devil. The pain served as a reminder that something went wrong.

The same week I slammed my head in the car, my friend, Mary, lost a baby she had been carrying in her womb for four months. This was the same Mary who carried the weight of Lucy's diagnosis with me a year earlier. When she lost the baby, I lost it. It broke my heart. It shattered hers.

I don't know why it happened.

She went in for a routine prenatal visit, something she had done dozens of times before between this baby and the three others she had already birthed. I don't know why this time a weight much heavier than a car door came out of nowhere
crashing into her
bringing pain
bringing tears
bringing a sense of disorientation.

Sometimes within the most normal ordinary rhythms of our life something happens that we didn't anticipate and it hurts. It hurts so terribly bad. It hurts worse than any physical pain we've endured.

From diagnoses to death and everything in between we experience hurt and disappointment in this world. Maybe you are carrying that kind of pain right now from a recent injury to your own soul.

In the weeks following Mary's miscarriage I watched her go about her daily life but I knew there was a tenderness to that injury of her soul, and it was certainly still throbbing with grief. Even if no one around could see, it was still there. I hugged her at preschool drop-off one morning and wished I could squeeze the pain right out of her, but I couldn't. What I could do was help her carry it, as she had helped me carry my own suffering.

Through word and deed, I could remind her that she would be ok, even though it didn't feel like it at the time. I could carry the hope of mourning turned to gladness for her until she could experience it for herself.

We get injured in this world. Some heavy object comes flying out of nowhere and presses pain deep into our souls. The death of a loved one, job loss, public failure, an unfaithful spouse, a diagnosis, a miscarriage...

Have any of these come slamming hard into you? Or maybe it's something else.

Tears come, but eventually, so does the healing.

And so we go on with carpooling and mowing the grass and cooking dinner and paying the bills - all the while still carrying that tenderness inside of us.

The injuries in this life can lead you back to healing, to a Healer, every single time if you let them. This kind of healing offers more than an ice pack and a band-aid. This kind of healing goes deep, restoring places in your spirit you didn't even know were sick or broken. With this kind of healing, the prognosis isn't that you will be 'back to normal' again soon but that you will be anything but 'normal' because of the depth of work that has been done inside of you. It's scary, and yet beautiful, all at the same time.

You may always carry the pain, but you don't have to carry it alone.

Your heart may always bear a scar but the tissue that grows back will be stronger than what was there before.

Whether in our own lives, or the lives of those around us, we are all called into the healing places - to carry or be carried.

One of the greatest gifts we can give to one another on this journey is permission.

Permission to cry and grieve
to hug and hope

to offer up our current life for the promise of something better no matter how painful the process of healing might be.

Healing isn't just about getting better than you are today. It's about getting even better than you were yesterday.

#typeonederland

Lucy,

I can't believe that its been 3 years since you were diagnosed with diabetes. During that time, God has built you into the strongest, most courageous 8 year old that I have ever met! I know that diabetes is tough, but you are tougher! I am so proud that you are my little girl.

Love,

Daddy

10/21/16

I gave her 3 balloons for the 3 years she has lived every aspect of her life with Type 1 Diabetes. Today we don't celebrate the disease, we celebrate the girl who is living beyond the disease. Her daddy said it well - diabetes is tough, but she is tougher. When I tucked her in bed tonight she said - 'Mommy, thank you for making this day so special.' Thank you for making our lives so special, Doodlebug. Happy Diaversary!

CHAPTER EIGHTEEN

Looking Back

I planned to go to bed an hour earlier but found myself wandering deeper and deeper back into our story. I have written it in snippets on my blog over the past seven years, beginning long before we ever knew life with Type 1 Diabetes. I sat at the kitchen table that night with my computer open, reading post after post of words and wonder depicting them - my people - the ones I share meals and germs and a roof with every day.

It was Lucy's 'birthday post' from the previous year that stopped me cold. It was the words I had written the day she turned five. They were my thoughts expressed just 5 months before we were admitted to the hospital. It was the wish I whispered over the cake and candles almost like a prophecy - *I want to see you be brave.*

The weight of the days we've lived since then pressed the tears clean out of me.

I saw my year-younger self, sitting at the keyboard with fingers dancing across the letters that would frame my daughter at five. There was not a single corner of my mind

that could have predicted the tumultuous year that would carry her to six. And yet from somewhere there came a light shining on that one word -
brave.

I picked up those shiny five letters and recognized their form, having seen it lived out in her little life ever since the day she was laid in my arms. I breathed one small word as big as I could into her life -
brave.

Our good God has made countless provisions for our family these past years but this one I nearly missed.

Before I saw the symptoms
and predicted the diagnoses
and heard the confirmation
and held her tight, as our world flipped upside down -
before any of that -
I began praying for it.
Brave.
And she is.

Perhaps God, in his infinite wisdom and mercy, prompted me to those prayers just as much for me as he did for her. With every prayer I have lifted for Lucy since her birthday on May 23, 2013 I saw the courage continue to grow.

When I watched them insert IV's into her arms
and needles into her fingertips
and insulin into her tissue,
I wanted it to be me but I knew it had to be her - the one

whose bright eyes never fade,
whose frame always stands strong,
whose heart is filled with courage.

I never wanted my baby to have to be that kind of brave
so young. God knew she would need to be so he
filled her,
covered her,
surrounded her,
and sealed her with His strength.
Because no five-year-old, no matter how brave, has it in
them to endure all that she has endured.

When I consider what she has carried, it breaks my heart
and then goes right ahead and fills it back up with joy.

She hasn't just carried pain and suffering. At 7 years old
she has carried the burden of two serious autoimmune
diseases and the difficult life that comes with them, but
she has also carried the strength and courage and grace
of the Spirit of the living God. I have no other explanation
for how she has endured and who she is becoming. So
early in life she has an eternal hope rooted deep inside of
her.

I don't think she will ever know another way of living, and
for that I am grateful.

Through every hormonal Graves' rage, every sobbing
question of 'why', every needle poke, every finger prick,
every gluten- free sugar-free dairy-free piece of food that
was different from everyone else's, one thing has

remained -
hope.

Even on the worst of days she has always recovered, always managed a smile and sometimes even uttered these words that speak hope straight to my own heart - *I can't wait for heaven, Mama. When I am there with Jesus I won't have diabetes anymore and I won't <u>ever</u> be sad.*

Her weakness. His strength.
Our Lucy. His light.

I have fought alongside her to keep it from going out – that fire that glows bright within. She rode into this ONEderland on the wings of brave, but she has set this world ablaze with hope. Every time I look at her I am nearly blinded by those dancing flames reflected in her face.

And so we always pray for the hope - that it would grow to consume her and others, like a hot, burning gift she would offer up. Finger to flame is painful, but watching the glow is magical and warm. She endures the pain and offers the magic. Everyone around her knows it's true - God is using her little life to prove

> *that suffering leads to endurance,*
> *endurance leads to strength of character,*
> *strength of character leads to confident hope,*
> *and hope, hope does not disappoint.*
> {Romans 5:3-5 NLT}

I have never seen the hard, beautiful truth of the apostle Paul's words more clearly - the words of a man who knew relentless suffering.

Every day God is revealing more of this child who calls me 'mama'. He is uncovering shiny pieces of who he has created her to be and I am the one with the coveted front row seat.

There is much to know and learn about type 1 diabetes. No two days are ever the same. But I refuse to be too distracted by researching her condition or overanalyzing her symptoms to just. be. her. mama.

To love her,
support her,
encourage her,
cheer for her,
teach her,
pray for her,
and leave the rest to God, in whom I place my complete trust.

Every child in this world has her own special needs and challenges, and every parent goes searching for answers at one time or another. But this mama is learning to rest in this truth - for all the things that I still don't know, what I do know is more than enough. I'm learning to be brave. It's her example I follow.

#typeonederland

Our Lucy, our light.
She is teaching us all what it looks like to truly love life.

CHAPTER NINETEEN

Get Well Soon

Lucy tore into the yellow envelope. It was one of dozens she received in the hospital at diagnosis. As she slid the card out I saw cute little bears alongside those familiar words.

Get Well Soon

Back when I didn't know much about type 1 diabetes, I probably would have sent that card too. It makes sense, right? If someone is in the hospital, you want her to get well so she can get home and get on with her life. People who care enough to send a card truly want what is best for you, but sometimes they don't understand that their wish is not a possibility. There was a time when I didn't understand.

There will be no 'getting well soon' for Lucy. Because there is no cure for type 1 diabetes she will live with that disease until, God willing, a cure is found.

As much as we have committed to staying positive and helping the management of T1D go as well as possible for our daughter, we also remember that her body is never completely well.

Every single day her fingers are poked and bled.

Every single day she has to keep up with the 2 pound medical device attached to her body.

Every single day she has to look at the carbohydrate count on the food she eats to determine if it's a good choice for her and, if so, how much insulin she will need to inject in order for her body to process it.

Every single day her body goes through the torment of blood sugar levels that skyrocket and then plummet leaving her both physically and emotionally affected.

Every single day she has to be awakened from her sleep so we can do a late night check of her blood sugar to ensure she doesn't need anything to safely sleep through the rest of the night.

As much as we 'deal with it' and commit to having a positive outlook, life with chronic illness is still incredibly difficult, both physically and emotionally. Lucy, and the other millions of people living with type 1 will never get well until we find a cure. So that's what we're after. Even her little brother has it at the top of his list of nightly prayers.
God, please cure Lucy's diabetes.
Please make her 'pancweas' work again.

Before Lucy began wearing an insulin pump she received between 4 and 6 insulin injections into her arms each day. Now we tell the pump how much insulin to administer into Lucy whenever she needs it. The port into which the insulin is delivered is injected into Lucy's little rear end. We change that port every three days which means that instead of 4 to 6 little injections every day, she gets one bigger one every three days.

In so many ways the pump has made all of our lives easier. We are grateful for technological advances such as those. But the pump is not perfect, so there have been new issues to address. Lucy has had to figure out how to wear it underneath and on top of clothes. She has also had to learn how to sleep with it on and maneuver in her daily activities while wearing it. She has done all of this with so much more ease and grace than I could have ever imagined.

Shortly after we had adjusted to life with a pump and Lucy seemed to be handling it as if it were 'no big deal', we had a malfunction. I freaked out because we had just transitioned to life with a pump. Injections were no longer part of our daily routine, but I knew we would have to temporarily go back to them until we could get the pump situation worked out. I freaked out because when you are living life with T1D everything is a delicate balance and when something disrupts that balance it is stressful. T1D cannot go unattended for even one hour without the potential for devastating consequences.

I took a few deep breaths and called Lucy's

endocrinologist. We figured out a game plan to get us through a couple of days before we could get the pump up and running again. Lucy had just gotten used to her pump so she didn't want to go back to injections, but she did. She quickly readjusted.

That first night following the malfunction Joey was out of town. Somewhere around midnight Lucy wandered into my room and whispered,
I had a bad dream Mommy.

Normally I would have walked her back to bed, rubbed her back and kissed all the scary thoughts away. But I had a big empty space next to me that night so, just as I had done two years prior, I pulled back the covers and she climbed in beside me.

She rolled over a couple of times to get comfortable and because she did not have the pump tubing attached to her she said quietly and happily,
Look Mommy! I can roll all around without getting tangled up. It's like I'm a regular girl again!

She said it with a smile, and although my own lips curled up to reflect hers, my mama heart cracked inside. I fought back tears because although she
shines bright and
fights hard and
adjusts well,
on some level type 1 diabetes always makes her different. It always keeps her just slightly separated from the freedom that comes with being a 'regular girl'. And

despite the fact that we know 'regular' is overrated, sometimes it would just be so much easier. To be rid of this disease would make her life so much easier.

It is the thorn in her flesh. It is the cross that she bears.

But it took a saint to endure the thorn,
and a savior to bear the cross,
so she is in good company.

Living her life with chronic disease will never be easy but hope shines brightest in the hard places –
and so she shines.

Epilogue

I am not a scientist or a doctor. I do not have a knack for organizing events or collecting donations. For many months following Lucy's diagnosis I struggled to find a way to give something back to the community that had given so much to our family.

I am a writer, so this book is my offering – to those who have supported us, and all those who need our support. Whether your life is affected by chronic illness or not, you have your own hard places. I don't want you to endure them alone. I want to sit across a table of shared tears and say, 'me too, friend.' These words are my small contribution to the world.

Maybe there is a place in your life where you would like to contribute something too. If we were sitting together on my back porch I would ask you about that. We might start by talking about your own hard places.

What are they? How have they positioned you, empowered you, changed you, equipped you to do something significant in this world?

I would encourage you to think outside of the box of 'regular'. I would help you gather up all your gifts and passions and see where they might take you.

Start small and dream big.

Do what is right in front of you right now.

Step by step, hand in hand, we can make an impact of eternal significance on this world.

What follows is my pep talk for you as you do what only you can do in your own small way in this big wide world full of hard places. It matters more than you know. You matter more than you know.

You were created.

You didn't just 'happen'.

Regardless of the circumstances surrounding your birth, you were thoughtfully made before you ever took your first breath.

You possess a unique
design
passion
purpose.

That sneaking, lying, no-good voice will try to tell you,
You don't have enough time.
You don't have enough talent.
You've missed your chance.
You're too old, too young, too busy, too whatever.
Your current circumstances are too difficult.

But there is a voice of truth that has been drowned out by the lies for too long. Can you hear it? Listen closely. It tells you 'that thing' is 'your thing'.

There are contributions to this world that will not be made if you don't make them.

There are things that need to be said, done, created, and offered in only the way you can say, do, create, and offer them.

There is purpose in both the seasons of triumph and

defeat.

Our good days and bad days carry purpose.

What if today wasn't just another day. What if today was the day we cleared our minds of the lies and got quiet enough to hear the sweet Spirit of truth calling us to
stand up
and
stand out.

Stop trying so hard to be regular.
You were created for more.

Close your eyes
spread your arms
tilt your face toward the sky
palms open wide
hearts open wider
falling into the person you were created to be,
difficult circumstances and all.

There is work to be done
light to be grown
love to be shared
grace to be offered
truth to be told
and art to be inspired.

You are needed.
You are necessary.

So let's not waste another moment paralyzed by the lies
and crippled by our circumstances.

Grab a hand,
take a step,
and lead hearts to a better place.

Deep breath in.
Deep breath out.

Let's get up and go somewhere new together.
We've been stuck in this old place too long.

*Friends, may you find hope in every hard place
and then offer it back up – again and again.*

what is Type 1 diabetes?

A chronic, autoimmune condition that occurs when the body's own immune system attacks and destroys the insulin-producing beta cells of the pancreas.

This attack leaves the pancreas with little or no ability to produce insulin, a hormone that regulates blood sugar.
sugar stays in the blood and can cause serious damage to organ systems.

People with T1D must inject or pump insulin into their bodies every day to carefully regulate blood sugar and stay alive.

T1D MEANS INSULIN DEPENDENCY FOR LIFE DIAGNOSED AT ANY AGE THREATENS DEVASTATING COMPLICTIONS DEMANDS METICULOUS PLANNING TO AVOID LIFE-THREATENING SITUATIONS

T1D is not T1D IS NOT A LIFESTYLE DISEASE SOMETHING YOU OUTGROW CONTAGIOUS, CAUSED BY SUGAR, PREVENTABLE CURABLE ...YET

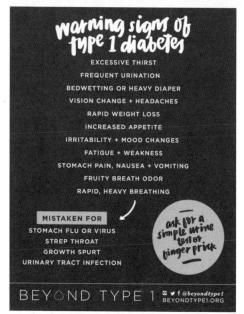

images and information provided by Beyond Type 1 – beyondtype1.org

~About the ~Author

Elizabeth is a storyteller, truth seeker, grace giver, and word weaver. She routinely chooses to read a book rather than put away laundry and visit with friends rather than do the grocery shopping. This makes her a terrible housekeeper and an average cook, but her people love her anyway. She may have dirty dishes piled in her kitchen sink but you'll always find fresh flowers on her windowsill. Elizabeth lives with her husband, Joey, and their children, Lucy and Oliver, on the edge of the woods in the college town of Clemson, South Carolina.

Connect with her at elizabethmaxon.com & @elizabethmaxon
To keep up with all the Onederland adventures search
#typeonederland

Also available from Elizabeth

For centuries people have connected themselves to God through the practice of spiritual disciplines, yet we feel overwhelmed at the prospect of integrating such disciplines into our own lives today. What if all that is really required is for us to simply - begin?

Beginnings are important. They determine how we will end.

The pages of "begin." will introduce you to the disciplines of solitude, silence, fasting, frugality, prayer, meditation, study, and worship, in a fresh new way. In addition to a few non-bossy suggestions about the art of implementing spiritual disciplines, you will also be given 40 readings and exercises to get you started right away.

Whether we are beginning a day.
beginning a project,
or beginning a new stage of life,

                           how we begin matters.

For more information: www.elizabethmaxon.com
#beginbook